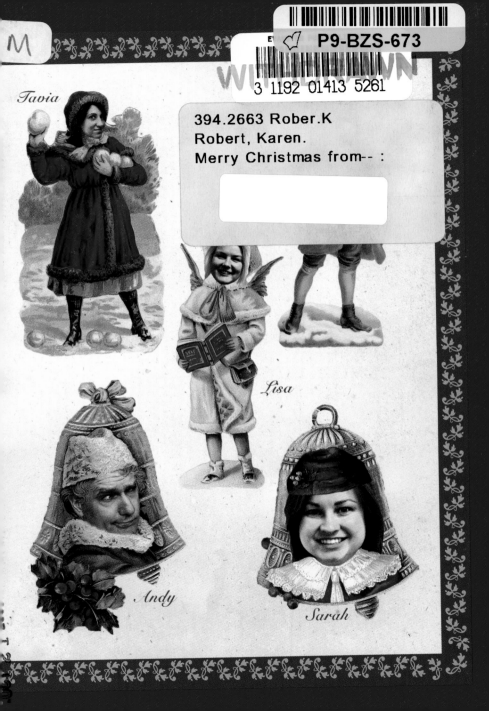

Tavia

Lisa

Andy

Sarah

TO: _____

MERRY CHRISTMAS FROM...

_____

MERRY CHRISTMAS FROM...

 150 Christmas Cards
You Wish
You'd Received

KAREN ROBERT

wm WILLIAM MORROW

An Imprint of HarperCollins*Publishers*

Submissions for future books are welcome at
www.merrychristmasfrom.com

HarperCollins books may be purchased for educational, business,
or sales promotional use. For information please write: Special Mar-
kets Department, HarperCollins Publishers, 10 East 53rd Street,
New York, NY 10022.

FIRST EDITION

Library of Congress Cataloging-in-Publication Data has been
applied for.

ISBN 978-0-06-147309-8

08 09 10 11 ov/scp 10 9 8 7 6 5 4 3 2 1

This book is dedicated to my mother, who has always been creative in everything she does, especially with her Christmas cards, and to my children, who have patiently posed for mine

INTRODUCTION

Sending out Christmas cards has changed in the last thirty years. With cheaper printing and more people going digital, it's now almost obligatory for people to send out pictures of their children, themselves, or even their pets. Usually parents feel compelled to dress up their children, haul them in front of a camera, and pray for good results. Some don't really care about being original or creative, some care but don't have the time, others have the time but not the inspiration. But we still love receiving these cards; it's a chance to catch up with friends, note how big their children are getting, and catch up on their lives. What we get the biggest kick out of, though, is receiving cards by our friends who somehow found the time, the inspiration, or the good luck to create cards that stand out on the mantelpiece—those cards that somehow rise above the rest and surprise us with their irrepressible creativity, offbeat uniqueness, or sheer genius. This book is about the cards that make us slap our foreheads and say, "Why didn't I think of that?"

I admit to being a bit obsessed with Christmas cards. I keep a notebook full of ideas, and months before Christmas I start thinking about our annual card far more than a normal person should. Probably it's my way of keeping my brain active while caring for four children. When I got the idea for this book I began in earnest tracking down the wonderful and wacky cards that I love; after looking through tens of thousands of people's personal cards, I finally selected these 150. My criteria were that they had to be extremely funny, strange, delightful, beautiful, or touching, and that they had to actually have been sent out as Christmas cards. None are commercial cards.

What I think makes these cards even more interesting is that they are not created for the masses; they are meant to be seen by only a select few before they are, more often than not, thrown away. In this way Christmas cards are almost an exclusive art form; they become even more precious when you realize how temporary they are meant to be. Many cards that I thought were amazing couldn't be included because the file or negative had been lost. This book documents some enchanting cards so that they are saved for others to see and be inspired by.

I would like to thank all of the people who created these cards for sharing them with us and allowing us a glimpse into their private lives. For some, allowing us to reprint their cards was a diffi-

cult decision, as if I were asking them to send their personal cards to absolute strangers; in a sense, that is indeed what I was asking of them. In fact, to further this idea, many people have included a holiday greeting. They all have a different way of saying it, but underneath, the message is the same: one of gratitude, warm wishes, or just an excuse to make someone laugh with joy. Isn't that what this time of year is all about?

It seems appropriate, therefore, that 50 percent of my proceeds for this book go to charity; the creativity found here does not belong to me, after all. The charity was an obvious choice: The Smile Train, which provides free surgery to children with cleft palates in the developing world. Since there are so many smiling children on the following pages, it seems right that this book provides other children with the ability to smile fully for the first time in their lives. Happiness is contagious, after all.

Merry Christmas,
Karen Robert

The Smile Train is an organization dedicated to providing free cleft lip and palate surgery to millions of children in the developing world. Without this surgery, most will never eat or speak properly. They are often not allowed to attend school or hold a job, and some are even abandoned. Without surgery, children in developing countries have no chance at a normal life.

Helping these children is the mission of The Smile Train. They provide free surgery for children who would otherwise not receive it. They have a unique approach of empowering local doctors in developing countries to perform surgeries that cost as little as $250 and take as little as forty-five minutes. This medical miracle gives these children not just a new smile but a second chance at life.

On the facing page is a Christmas card from The Smile Train showing just a few of the children they have helped. For more information go to www.smiletrain.org or call 1-877-543-7645.

TheSmileTrain
Changing The World One Smile At A Time.

This holiday season,
somewhere in the world, a little kid is smiling.

You should be too.

Do not open until Christmas.

Let it snow.

Blessed are they who see Christmas through the eyes of a child.

Merry Christmas!

Peace on Earth.

Hoe, hoe, hoe.

Christmas is in the details.

Merry Christmas and a Happy New Year.

I peaked with my first Christmas card.
Happy Holidays from Iceland.

To my favorite elf. From Santa's little helper.

Family, we've never been closer.
Happy Holidays.

Peace and brotherly love.

"Christmas, children, is not a date. It is a state of mind."
—Mary Ellen Chase

Merry Christmas from Capri.

Joy to the world.

Wishing you the joy of new things in the holiday season and beyond.

Have a swell Christmas.

OUTSHOP OUTWRAP

SURVIVOR

CHRISTMAS

OUTTRIM

Shopping List

STEVEN
RUDT
ELLA
MOM
OTIS
CO
TIM
MARE
ROO
NEF
NAT
GE

. . . hope you're surviving yours.

Have a *very Merry* Christmas, from all of us.

Happy Christmas.

Merry Christmas from Santa's little helpers.

Merry Christmas.

Merry Christmas and Happy Holidays from the Rapscallion Russells.

All I want for Christmas is treats.

Do these antlers make me look fat?

Sure... laugh it up. Dog in a Santa hat. Never gets old. Truly. I chuckle every time.

In fact, whenever I'm doing something totally awful like playing in the park or tormenting the cat, I like to think of this time and savor the joy.

I can't wait until it's that time of year when I wear the hat and you eat the cookies. Marvelous.

Here's wishing you all the cookies you want this holiday season.

Happy Holidays.

". . . and so, during these holiday seasons, we thank our blessings."
—George W. Bush

, ♥, and ☺.

MARY AND THE THREE WISE MEN

TIMBUKTU, MALI   Nov '06

May all your holiday wishes come true.

2 0 0 5

If we don't run into a large steel ship, if we don't drown in the storm or get soaked in the rain, if there is no mutiny on the ship, then we we will reach our destination.

Don't talk to strangers in the New Year—dance with them.

I spy a little red wagon, a pair of penguins and the name Riley; five candy kisses, a toy soldier, a hidden Mickey, a Jedi Knight and Tanner; three stars, a doe, a deer, a saddle, and two angels.

Wishing you a perfect Christmas.

The Beam Team

Happy Holidays from TQ Express.

Santa's staff meeting.

Concerned about the whole "naughty or nice" thing... Kaitlyn and Nathan move on to Plan B.

For many years after the incident, Lauren remained on Santa's "naughty" list.

Capture the Holiday Spirits!
Love, The April Family.

Merry Christmas from Santa's little . . . uh, helpers.

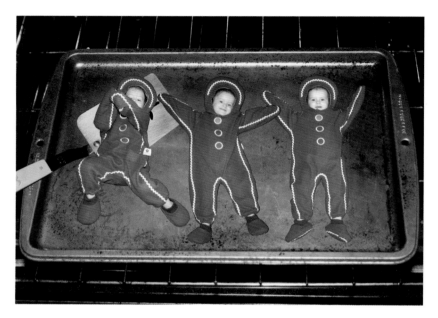

Gingerbread triplets lined up in a row, sending
holiday greetings to all that we know.

Happy Holidays!

DAILY VARIETY

$2.50
FRIDAY
DECEMBER 1, 2000
PERIODICALS POSTAGE PAID

LOS ANGELES ■ NEW YORK ■ NEWSPAPER

WILSON KIDS NIX X-MAS CARD PIX

Tyke Strikers Foil AnnualTradition

By HOLLY DAY

SANTA MONICA - These days, it's anything but a silent night at the Wilson residence, where the sidewalks resound with chants of "NO-NO-NO" instead of "HO-HO-HO." Tired of year after year with no residuals, these two tyro protestors refuse to take part in this year's X-mas Card Fest, derailing plans for an interactive, multi-media pop-up card that the elder Wilsons were calling, "Outrageous! Our best effort yet!" Talks have stalled, after both sides left the negotiation table (it was after bedtime) leaving little hope for an agreement before the postal service deadline. *Turn to page 3*

INSIDE

6 K-9 crosses line

Pet pooch poses for pix despite taunts and jeers from peeved picketers.
....

7 Parents call a time out

Visit the Wilson's X-Mas website at www.hillsandhoads.com

Revolting children.

happy holidays

God made her for us. . . . Merry Christmas.

Happy Hollandaise.

Sending sweet sugarplum kisses this holiday season.

Wishing you happy holidays and a *GOODYEAR*

Sandoval '04

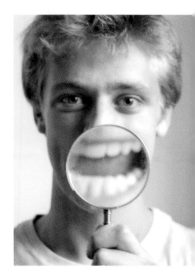

Have a fairy Merry Christmas.

Fishing you a Merry Christmas

Have an Incredible New Year.

... and a great New Year.

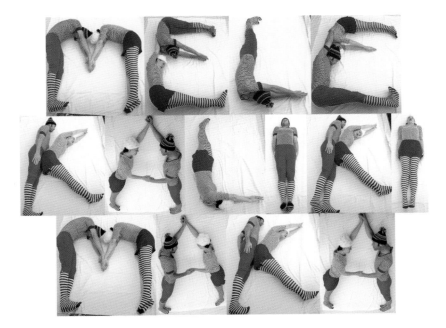

MELEKALIKIMAKA

(Merry Christmas from Hawaii)

The children were nestled all snug round our heads,
while visions of holidays filled the homestead. . . .

As we shifted our heads and seats on the ground, down the
"chimney" our littlest came with a bound!

Wishing you a very Merry Christmas.

Still cleaning up after last year's #$*& . . .
For a sparkling New Year.

Merry Christmas

xoxoxoxo
Steve

"The only thing you don't want to find in your stocking
on Christmas morning is your husband."
—Joan Rivers

(FROM 1952) May the joy of this holiday season be reflected
in your eyes and in your smile.

(FROM 1971) Happy leap year.

Wake up, it's a new year!

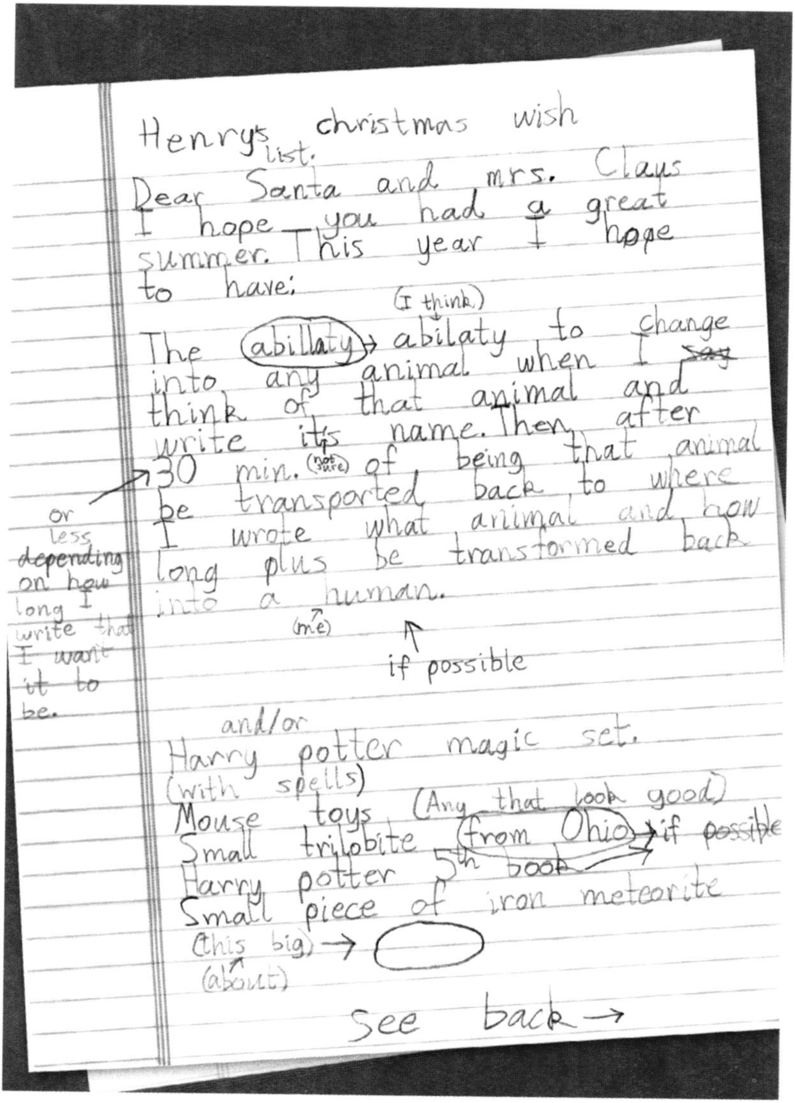

Henry's christmas wish
list.

Dear Santa and mrs. Claus
I hope you had a great
summer. This year I hope
to have:

(I think.)

The ~~abillaty~~ → abilaty to change
into any animal when I
think of that animal and
write it's name. Then, after
30 min. (note) of being that animal
be transported back to where
I wrote what animal and how
long plus be transformed back
into a human.

or less depending on how long I write that I want it to be.

(me)

if possible

and/or
Harry potter magic set.
(with spells)
Mouse toys (Any that look good)
Small trilobite (from Ohio) → if possible
Harry potter 5th book
Small piece of iron meteorite
(this big) → ◯
(about)

See back →

Wishing you the best holiday season ever (if possible).

The holidays are better when shared with friends.

Q: What's in the bag?
A: A melted snowman

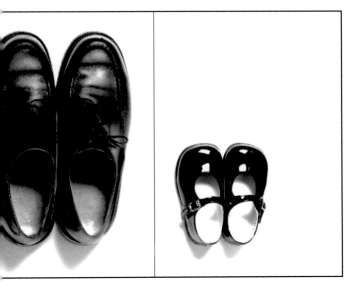

Merry Christmas, best wishes from Norway.

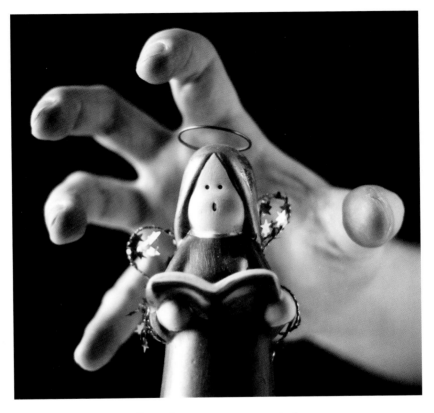

Surprises come unexpected.

Oh what fun it is to ride. . . .

Merry Christmas from airmen of the 332nd sq., Iraq.

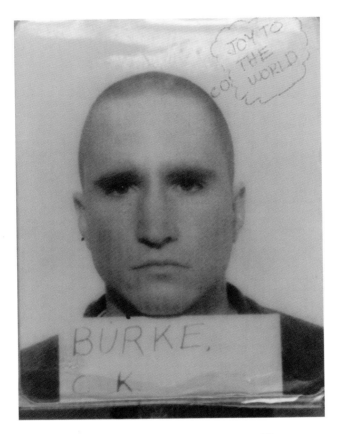

Message from Master Gunnery Sergeant Hartman:
Happy Birthday, dear Jesus.

Wishing You a

Merry Christmas

and Happy New Year

From Matt

. . . and a Merry Christmas to you.

Happy Holidays from our family to yours.

"...HE HADN'T STOPPED CHRISTMAS FROM COMI

FROM THE **WHO**S AT RETAIL CONSTRUCTION SERVIC

SOMEHOW OR OTHER, IT CAME JUST THE SAME!"

A JOYOUS HOLIDAY AND A PROSPEROUS NEW YEAR.

Happy Holidays from TQ Express.

Professional AirFreight...

...Come Fly With Us!

119

SEATTLE
SEAHAWKS

FROM HALL & COMPANY

121

Happy Holidays . . . seriously.

Happy Holidays from the Flakes.

HAPPY HOLIDAYS
FROM MEG & TOM.

Happy Holidays from Hall and Company.

Peace.

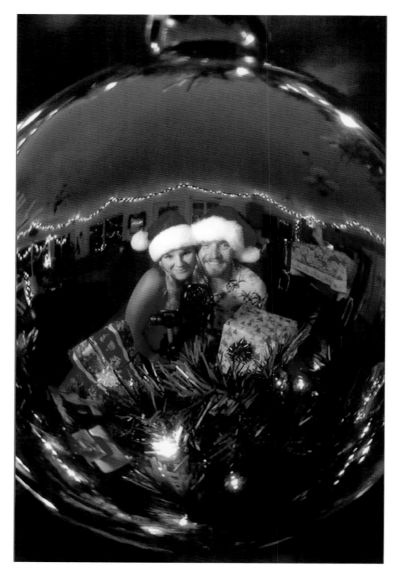

Melekalikimaka.

Merry Christmas from me to you. My wish for you is to have a glorious holiday filled with joy, happiness, and laughter. And I pray that, come what may, the laughter will last throughout the coming year.

Happy Holidays from Fred, Thor, Napoleon Dynamite, and all the other dogs of Central Texas Dachshund Rescue.

Merry Christmas from the Redhed Ornament Manufacturing Co.
Happily producing quality homemade ornaments since 1999.

Hope your holidays are heavenly.

May the New Year bring you moments to cherish and
peace to enjoy them.

Walking in a Winter Wonderland

'Tis the season
for miracles

Wishing you your own New Year of miracles.

Fleas Navidad.

From our sweet home to yours, Merry Christmas.

Peace and Joy

Wishing you and your family warmth and wonder
throughout the season and New Year.

Wishing you a year full of joyful surprises.

we two kings and a princess...

and then there

were tree

God Jul!

60452/6

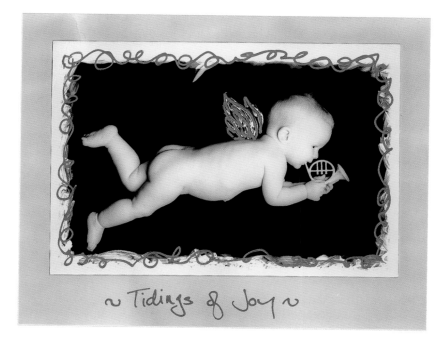

~ Tidings of Joy ~

Today in the town of David, a Savior has been born to you.
He is Christ the Lord.
Merry Christmas.

From Bouti and Leo, a Merry Mediterranean Christmas.

With the hopes of capturing
the ideal beamish image of
the beamish boy in
holiday regalia for a
holiday card, we draped him
in Christmas lights, and he held
a candle, wearing his best
suit jacket and a red
Santa hat, outside in the
deep December dark
that seeped into this night.
Merry Christmas to all.

Dear Santa, I can explain.

Have a holly, jolly Christmas.

May love and joy be piled upon you as
we celebrate the season of Christ's birth.

I have a list of folks I know all written in a book,
And every year at Christmastime I go and take a look.
So that is when I realize these names are each a part
Not of the book they're written on, but of my very heart.

For each name stands for someone who has crossed my path sometime,
And in that meeting they've become the "Rhythm and the Rhyme."
So while it sounds fantastic for me to make this claim—
I really feel I am composed of each remembered name.

And while you may not be aware of any special link
Just know that you have shaped my life more than you'd ever think.
For once you've met somebody the years cannot erase,
The memory of a pleasant word or of a friendly face.

So never think my Christmas cards are just a mere routine
Of names upon a Christmas list forgotten in between.
And when I send a Christmas card that is addressed to you,
It's because you're on that list of folks I am indebted to.

For I am but a total of the many folks I've met.
You happen to be some of those I simply can't forget.
So whether I have known you for many years or few,
In some way you have had a part in shaping things I do.

And every year when Christmas comes I realize anew,
The Greatest Gift that life can give is knowing folks like you.
Then may the Spirit of Christmas that forever and ever endures,
Leave its warmest, richest blessing in the hearts of You and Yours.

—*Winnie Pearl "Peggy" Hale, 1988*

Acknowledgments

At the risk of sounding like I am giving a speech at the Oscars, I am grateful to the following people: Karen Duffy, who put a fire under me and got me to start this book; David Mansfield, who was the first to sit and talk me through it; Henry Ferris at William Morrow, my hero, who got this all started; and Cassie Jones, my editor, who finished the job with a little help from Johnathan Wilber. To my husband, Marc, for his supportive shoulder; to my children, Oscar, Nicholas, Eloise, and Evelyn, who gave up many hours of Mom time; and to Claudia Bermudez, who played Mom for me when I couldn't. I'd also like to thank my brother, Andy Kaynor, who designed my website and taught me how little I know about computers.

But mostly I am grateful to all the people who made these wonderful Christmas cards. Each card represents countless hours of time spent behind cameras, in front of computers, making costumes, painting feet, finding props, making sand castles, or cutting and pasting. Thank you.

". . . and to all a good night."

CREDITS

Endpapers: the *Merry Christmas from . . .* book team, concept by Greg Simpson, designed by Andy Kaynor, Victorian cards provided by Ann Kiesler; **half-title page:** design © Betsy Cordes; **title page:** Stefani Greene; **copyright:** Andrea Wolff; **dedication:** Karen Robert; **6:** photograph by Tanya Malott, design by Karen Robert; **8/9:** photograph by Michael Donnelly, design by Karen Robert, graphics by Andy Kaynor; **11:** courtesy of the Smile Train; **12 and 13:** Marc Battaglia; **14:** Greta Mansour; **15:** James David Phenicie; **16 and 17:** Hugo Burnand; **18:** Anthea Bosch; **19:** Jay Shoots; **20 and 21:** Andrea Wolff; **22:** photograph by Ed Chiquitucto, design by Dan Driscoll; **23:** photograph by Sean Randall, design by Sean and Tracy Randall; **24:** photograph by Gudjon Jonsson, design by Guomundur Johansson; **25:** Michael James; **26:** Chrissy White; **27:** J. Cam Barker; **28:** photograph by Alicia Kuehn, designed by Adam Stevens/Atom design Lab; **29:** Carol Rice; **30:** Eric L. Gaddy; **31:** Jay Shoots; **32:** Andrea D'Agostino; **33:** Tanya Malott; **34:** © Barbara Vaughn Photography; **35:** photograph by Archive Holdings Inc./Getty Images, design by Simon Abrams; **36:** design by Doug Kochmanski; **37:** design by Hillary Wilson; **38:** design by Matthias Plunkett; **39:** Melissa Forman and Michael Jewell; **40:** photograph by Mike Warren, design by Bob Smith; **41:** created by Phillip Baird; **42:** Julie Mixon; **43:** Mark Sanders; **44:** Brandon Stirling; **45:** Caterina Giordano; **46:** Hollie Rockwell; **47:** Lyn Topinka; **48:** Marc Wensel; **49:** design by Simon Abrams; **50:** Sylvie Mulcahey; **51:** Tanya Malott; **52:** Karen Robert; **53:** photograph by Lucinda Wierenga, sand castle built by Dave Downs; **54:** design by David and Mary Creighton; **55:** Ken Trombotore and Jenny Boyd; **56 and 57:** Zoya Frolova and Janis Jakobson; **58:** Chris Powell; **59:** Jeff Holmes Photography; **60:** photo collage by Mike Newton; **61:** photograph by Sean Browne, design by Kari and Sean Browne; **62:** design by Trey Walker; **63:** Patrick Fitzgerald; **64:** photograph and design by David S. April; **65:** created by John and Willma Redhed; **66:** photograph and design by Patricia Roush; **67:** photograph and design by Chris Powell; **68:** design © Betsy Cordes; **69:** Hugo Burnand; **70:** Tiffany Brubaker Photography; **71:** Frank C. Coffin III; **72:** Andrea Wolff; **73:** Terriel Lara; **74:** Vanessa Disario; **75:** Carrie Sandoval; **76/77:** Bunty Kingham; **78:** Julie Lemberger; **79:** Clare Fisher; **80:** Natalie Davies; **81:** Ben and Riddell Scott; **82:** photograph by Sean Randall, design by Tracy and Sean Randall; **83:** Brindon Calmes and Becky Calmes; **84/85:** © Barbara Vaughn Photography; **86:** photograph and design by Brian Bowker; **87:** photograph and design by Anya Garrett; **88/89:** Julian Ingram; **90:** © Barbara Vaughn Photography; **91:** Steve Stanton; **92:** photograph and design by

For further contact information on the
designers and photographers, please go to:

www.merrychristmasfrom.com

Cassie

Johnathan

Merry Christmas From...

Karen

Henry

Susan